BOUNTIFUL BLESSINGS

31 DAY DEVOTIONAL

BOUNTIFUL BLESSINGS

31 DAY DEVOTIONAL

by DeAngela S. Reid
© 2019

Copyright © 2019
by DeAngela S. Reid

All rights reserved. No part of this book may be reprinted or reproduced in any form or by any electronic, mechanical, or other means, now known or hereafter invented, including photocopy, recording, and information storage and retrieval, without permission in writing from the publisher.

ISBN: 978-0-9996746-8-0
Library of Congress Control Number: 2019907421

Designed & Published by:
The Solid Foundation Group, LLC
Atlanta, Georgia
www.TheSolidFoundationGroup.com

Cover Designed by:
Amber Totten, Freshwind Graphics

Printed in the United States of America

DEDICATION

In loving memory of Bishop Gary Bernard Jones

INTRODUCTION

Bountiful Blessings was written to inspire individuals to spend some intimate time with God daily. In addition, it was written to address practical issues in life and to guide people to the life that God intended for us to have…the abundant life.

A Poetic Moment…

BOUNTIFUL BLESSINGS

Amazing how one day we go from chasing down blessings to blessings chasing us down and running us over.
Reward after reward just for being obedient to our great Jehovah.
That proverbial window from heaven has finally opened up.
Blessings come down and overflow your cup.
Bountiful means numerous, abundant, generous and ample.
What you have seen so far is only a sample.
Give praise for everything He has done in your life but most of all thank Him for being your peace in the midst of strife.

TABLE OF CONTENTS

TIME WELL SPENT	1
ATTITUDE ADJUSTMENT	2
A COMPASSIONATE WALK	3
WISE CHOICES	4
HUMILITY	5
TOTAL COMMITMENT	6
JOY	7
BE ENCOURAGED	8
SPEAK LIFE	9
THE GOODNESS OF GOD	10
HOPE	11
PEACE BE STILL	11

FAITH	13
FAITH WITHOUT WORKS	14
MOVING FORWARD	15
WALKING BILLBOARD	16
POWER OF PRAYER	17
QUALIFYING	18
PATIENCE	19
THE GOOD STEWARD	20
GLASS HALF FULL	21
FORGIVENESS	22
BEING STILL	23
OBEDIENCE	24
TAKE COURAGE	25
TAMING YOUR THOUGHTS	26
THE MESSENGER	27
FREE AT LAST	28
APPEARANCES	29
KEEP DREAMING	30
LIGHTEN UP	31

DAY 1
TIME WELL SPENT

Matthew 6:33 (KJV)
But seek ye first the kingdom of God, and his righteousness;
and all these things shall be added unto you.

Time seems to be the only commodity here on earth that cannot be replaced. It is wise to use it with discretion. There is an old expression used "we make time for the things that are important to us". This is so very true because everything else gets a great or not so great excuse. Take some time to deliberately spend with God because quality time can make or break a relationship.

Today's Sentence Prayer
Dear Lord, please help me prioritize my life, make the main things the main things and show me ways to cultivate my beautiful relationship with you. In the precious name of Jesus, I pray... Amen.

DAY 2
ATTITUDE ADJUSTMENT

James 4:7 (KJV)
Submit yourselves therefore to God.
Resist the devil, and he will flee from you.

Quite candidly, the circumstances of life are going to happen as long as you are on this side of heaven, so that basically means your reaction to life's circumstances are indeed critical. Your attitude in life can make your events better or worse and it really is all up to you. Do not allow your attitude to be so toxic that you cannot see any sunshine ever. Resist the devil's attempts to annihilate your sunshine.

Today's Sentence Prayer
Dear Lord, please help me with my attitude adjustment and with my reactions to life's actions that I may resist the devil so that he will flee and not hinder the sunshine in my life. In Jesus' name, I pray...Amen.

DAY 3
A COMPASSIONATE WALK

1 John 3:17 (KJV)
But whoso hath this world's good, and seeth his brother have need, and shutteth up his bowels of compassion from him, how dwelleth the love of God in him?

1 John 4:20 (KJV)
If a man says, I love God, and hateth his brother, he is a liar: for he that loveth not his brother whom he hath seen, how can he love God whom he hath not seen?

Have you lost the ability to care, be sympathetic or empathetic as it pertains to other people? You are not dwelling on an island where other people do not exist. You should care about the circumstances of others and realistically speaking that does not mean you have to consume your life with the burdens of the entire world because YOU ARE NOT GOD! But by all means you should care. You should help how and when you can and leave the rest to God.

Today's Sentence Prayer
Dear Lord, please help me to be a compassionate person that I may show empathy and sympathy toward my fellow man. In Jesus' name, I pray... Amen.

DAY 4
WISE CHOICES

2 John 1:8 (KJV)
Look to yourselves, that we lose not those things which we have wrought, but that we receive a full reward.

Psalm 1 (KJV)
Blessed is the man that walketh not in the counsel of the ungodly

---

You should avoid making rash and impulsive decisions especially concerning major things. Seek wise council from someone grounded in his or her spiritual walk. They do not have to necessarily be a seminary student but they should have a relationship where they spend personal time with God so they can pray about your situation and get an answer. By all means be careful of whom you let speak over your circumstances in life.

Today's Sentence Prayer
Dear Lord, please develop in me strong self-control and discipline that I may make wise decisions in my life. In Jesus' name, I pray...Amen.

DAY 5
HUMILITY

Luke 14:11 (KJV)
For whosoever exalteth himself shall be abased;
and he that humbleth himself shall be exalted.

Humility is the quality of never being arrogant, and meekness is a wonderful characteristic to possess. You should be in the habit of letting others praise you, your work or your ideas rather than you praising yourself. It is wonderful to have great self-esteem. After all, you are royalty; but, be careful not to let confidence transform into arrogance.

Today's Sentence Prayer
Dear Lord, please help to keep a humble spirit no matter what circumstances come my way. In Jesus' name, I pray...Amen.

DAY 6
TOTAL COMMITMENT

Colossians 3:23 (KJV)
And whatsoever ye do, do it heartily, as to the Lord,
and not unto men.

We as Christians are commanded to work as unto the Lord and that is basically what total commitment is all about. You have to decide not to procrastinate so that you can get started and then you have to decide to finish what you start. Total commitment is a decision to operate in excellence so you will hear those blessed words "Well done my good and faithful servant".

Today's Sentence Prayer
Dear Lord, Bless me to be released from a spirit of procrastination as well as give me the wherewithal to finish every endeavor that I start and anoint me to operate in excellence. In Jesus' name, I pray…Amen.

DAY 7
JOY

Romans 15:13 (KJV)
Now the God of hope fill you with all joy and peace in believing, that ye may abound in hope, through the power of the Holy Ghost.

Joy is not disbursed by the world but rather by the living God. It is the "thing" that allows you to smile even when your world is in distress. It cannot be bought, sold or traded because just like salvation it is a gift from God Himself.

Today's Sentence Prayer
Dear Lord, sometimes I seem to allow the circumstances of this world to affect my joy, please restore it and take me back to that joyful place in YOU! In Jesus' name, I pray...Amen.

DAY 8
BE ENCOURAGED

Philippians 4:13 (KJV)
I can do all things through Christ which strengtheneth me.

Life has this way of knocking us down but you should be encouraged to get back up and not only start things again but to trust God again, after all, you can all things through Christ who strengthens you.

Today's Sentence Prayer
Dear Lord, I come to you now for a dose of divine encouragement; Life can be pretty hard to deal with but help me remember that I am not alone and with you all things are possible. In Jesus' name, I pray…Amen.

DAY 9
SPEAK LIFE

Proverbs 18:21 (KJV)
Death and life are in the power of the tongue: and they that love it shall eat the fruit thereof.

It is vital that you tame your tongue to speak those things that are positive rather than negative. Scripture tells us that life and death are in the power of the tongue and it is so very true. "Whether you say you can or can't, you are right" ~ Author unknown

Today's Sentence Prayer
Dear Lord, please help me to tame my tongue in such a manner that I refuse to speak negativity because I deliberately choose to speak life. In Jesus' name, I pray...Amen.

DAY 10
THE GOODNESS OF GOD

Psalm 27:13 (KJV)
I had fainted, unless I had believed to see the goodness of the LORD in the land of the living.

So many Christians are under the erroneous belief that they will only see God's goodness when they get to heaven. You can and should expect to see His goodness right here in the land of the living. Pray with expectancy and walk in faith and by all means keep your eyes open so you can see His goodness.

Today's Sentence Prayer
Dear Lord, I pray that you will show your goodness right here in the land of the living, for you can do anything but fail. In Jesus' name, I pray…Amen.

DAY 11
HOPE

Proverbs 10:28 (KJV)
The hope of the righteous shall be gladness:
but the expectation of the wicked shall perish.

Proverbs 13:12 (KJV)
Hope deferred maketh the heart sick:
but when the desire cometh, it is a tree of life.

Believing that things can get better is what hope is in a nutshell. Quite candidly, hope is what keeps so many people from being depressed; seeing a glimmer of light at the end of the tunnel. Hold on to your hope and keep pressing towards your beautiful future.

Today's Sentence Prayer
Dear Lord, please help me to both see and hold on to my hope for my future. In Jesus's name, I pray...Amen.

DAY 12
PEACE BE STILL

Luke 8:23-25 (KJV)
23 But as they sailed he fell asleep: and there came down a storm of wind on the lake; and they were filled with water, and were in jeopardy. 24 And they came to him, and awoke him, saying, Master, master, we perish. Then he arose, and rebuked the wind and the raging of the water: and they ceased, and there was a calm. 25 And he said unto them, Where is your faith? And they being afraid wondered, saying one to another, What manner of man is this! for he commandeth even the winds and water, and they obey him.

We serve an awesome God who has the power to calm the rocky storms of our lives. Life can really be filled with turbulence at times and we are simply expected to roll with the punches so we need the Lord to say peace be still.

Today's Sentence Prayer
Dear Lord, please give me the strength to make it through the storms of my life. In Jesus' name, I pray…Amen.

DAY 13
FAITH

Hebrews 11:1 (KJV)
Now faith is the substance of things hoped for,
the evidence of things not seen.

Having faith is not always easy because it requires believing in something you cannot see or touch, so this could be a struggle. Embrace a spirit of expectancy, grab a hold of your faith, and simply dare to believe.

Today's Sentence Prayer
Dear Lord, I thank you for the measure of faith that you have blessed me with and I pray that you will fortify me as I dare to believe. In Jesus' name, I pray…Amen.

DAY 14
FAITH WITHOUT WORKS

James 2:26 (KJV)
For as the body without the spirit is dead,
so faith without works is dead also.

Actions speak louder than words rings true in the sense of saying you believe but your actions display they complete and sheer opposite. Example 1: You are believing God for rain but you always leave your umbrella at home. Example 2: You are believing God for new employment but you don't complete any applications. Simply do your part and leave the rest to God.

Today's Sentence Prayer
Dear Lord, Please help me to act out my faith so that I am offering more than mere lip service. In Jesus' name, I pray…Amen.

DAY 15
MOVING FORWARD

Philippians 3:14 (KJV)
I press toward the mark for the prize of the high calling of God in Christ Jesus.

Moving forward requires day-by-day faith and growing in His word. We cannot afford to be spiritually or emotionally paralyzed because God has work for us to do as we dwell here on earth. Relinquish the past, embrace the present and keep moving forward.

Today's Sentence Prayer
Dear Lord, please help me to let go of my past so that I can keep pressing my way towards my blessed future. In Jesus' name, I pray…Amen.

DAY 16
WALKING BILLBOARD

2 Corinthians 5:20 (KJV)
Now then we are ambassadors for Christ,
as though God did beseech you by us: we pray you in
Christ's stead, be ye reconciled to God.

As Christians, we are representatives for the kingdom of God. We are by no means perfect and we are not expected to be great representatives within our own strength but rather with the power of the Holy Spirit. People are watching your life to see the works of this Mighty God you serve.

Today's Sentence Prayer
Dear Lord, please help me to represent your kingdom in absolute excellence. In Jesus' name, I pray…Amen.

DAY 17
POWER OF PRAYER

James 5:16 (KJV)
Confess your faults one to another, and pray one for another, that ye may be healed. The effectual fervent prayer of a righteous man availeth much.

Prayer has the power to change circumstances, people, outlooks and much more in life. It is a powerful tool that God has equipped us with but it is up to you to use the tool. It is not about you forming the perfect words but rather humbling yourself and having a genuine conversation with God.

Today's Sentence Prayer
Dear Lord, Speak to my heart and hear my cry unto you and if this is not the day that my circumstances are going to change, grant me coping grace to get through my trials. In Jesus' name, I pray...Amen.

DAY 18
QUALIFYING

Ephesians 2:8-9 (KJV)
8 For by grace are ye saved through faith; and that not of yourselves: it is the gift of God:
9 Not of works, lest any man should boast.

Romans 3:23 (KJV)
For all have sinned, and come short of the glory of God;

Unlike the organizations here on earth, salvation is not something that you have to qualify for but rather it is a beautiful gift from God through His beautiful son. Young, old, rich or poor, no matter the color of your skin as long as you have truly accepted this beautiful gift into your heart you have a V.I.P. pass into heaven.

Today's Sentence Prayer
Dear Lord, I just simply want to thank you for the beautiful gift in the person of your son Jesus. It is in Jesus' name, I pray…Amen.

DAY 19

PATIENCE

Galatians 6:9 (KJV)
And let us not be weary in well doing:
for in due season we shall reap, if we faint not.

Accepting delay is not easy for everyone, in fact for some of us humans, this is not our strong suit but nevertheless it is wise to exercise patience in life. It is something you can pray for but let me warn you that traffic may move a little slower.

Today's Sentence Prayer
Dear Lord, please help me to be wise and exercise patience throughout this journey called life. In Jesus' name, I pray...Amen.

DEANGELA S. REID

DAY 20
THE GOOD STEWARD

1 Corinthians 4:2 (KJV)
Moreover it is required in stewards, that a man be found faithful.

Matthew 25:21 (KJV)
His lord said unto him, Well done, thou good and faithful servant: thou hast been faithful over a few things, I will make thee ruler over many things: enter thou into the joy of thy lord.

Good stewardship is being wise with the things that God has assigned you to manage. This would include your family, gifts and talents as well. God has plenty of confidence in you to give you so many things to manage but do not just manage them rather manage them with excellence.

Today's Sentence Prayer
Dear Lord, please give me the wherewithal to manage your things with excellence. In Jesus' name, I pray...Amen.

DAY 21
GLASS HALF FULL

Romans 12:2 (KJV)
And be not conformed to this world: but be ye transformed by the renewing of your mind, that ye may prove what is that good, and acceptable, and perfect, will of God.

Being optimistic is an artform that not everyone can grab a hold of especially in such a skeptical world. Some of us humans have the ability to point out that proverbial silver lining that every cloud has. Faith in itself requires a touch of optimism just to believe that certain things can in fact happen, especially when you cannot see them.

Today's Sentence Prayer
Dear Lord, help me to always look at life through the proper lenses so that I can see my glass as half full. In Jesus' name, I pray…Amen.

DAY 22
FORGIVENESS

Matthew 18:21-22 (KJV)
21 Then came Peter to him, and said, Lord, how oft shall my brother sin against me, and I forgive him? till seven times? 22 Jesus saith unto him, I say not unto thee, Until seven times: but, Until seventy times seven.

You must realize that forgiveness is for your healing not for the person that you need to forgive, because grudges weigh you down and keep your heart burdened. So, free yourself and please release that. Learn to forgive yourself too because God already has done so.

Today's Sentence Prayer
Dear Lord, please help release the burden of unforgiveness so that I can forgive everyone that I feel has wronged me in some way. In Jesus' name, I pray…Amen.

DAY 23
BEING STILL

Psalm 46:10 (KJV)
Be still, and know that I am God: I will be exalted among the heathen, I will be exalted in the earth.

Being still is not always an easy thing to do for many of us because we see being still and sitting idle synonymously but they really are not the same thing. Sitting idle is being so complacent to the point where you have no desire to move forward in your life while being still is doing your part then waiting patiently for God to do His part and letting Him show the Almighty God that He is indeed.

Today's Sentence Prayer
Dear Lord, please help me to be still so that can see your greatness moving in my life. In Jesus' name, I pray...Amen.

DAY 24
OBEDIENCE

Proverbs 21:3 (KJV)
To do justice and judgment is more acceptable
to the LORD than sacrifice.

Obedience to God is all about dos and don'ts. It is about completing those things that God has told you to do, while conversely not doing those things that God has told you were off limits. In essence, obedience is following His divine instructions.

Today's Sentence Prayer
Dear Lord, please help me to walk daily with a spirit of obedience so that I may live a life pleasing in your sight. In Jesus' name, I pray…Amen.

DAY 25
TAKE COURAGE

Joshua 1:9 (KJV)
Have not I commanded thee? Be strong and of a good courage; be not afraid, neither be thou dismayed: for the LORD thy God is with thee whithersoever thou goest.

God has not given you the spirit of fear so if you are feeling fearful you can release that because it does not belong to you. Be brave because there is absolutely no problem or situation that is bigger than Almighty God.

Today's Sentence Prayer
Dear Lord, please endow me with courage to make it through the various circumstances of life. In Jesus' name, I pray…Amen.

DAY 26
TAMING YOUR THOUGHTS

Philippians 4:8 (KJV)
Finally, brethren, whatsoever things are true, whatsoever things are honest, whatsoever things are just, whatsoever things are pure, whatsoever things are lovely, whatsoever things are of good report; if there be any virtue, and if there be any praise, think on these things.

Think on all the positive things that you have and also think on how grateful you are for the doors that God has closed for you that could have very well been the death of you. Take those negative thoughts captive and hold on to the truth and power of God's word.

Today's Sentence Prayer
Dear Lord, please grant me the ability to take all my negative thoughts captive and focus on the positive things in life. In Jesus' name, I pray...Amen.

DAY 27
THE MESSENGER

Romans 10:17 (KJV)
So then faith cometh by hearing, and hearing by the word of God.

God has called and ordained many anointed men and women to preach the gospel to a dying world. We are commanded in His word to revere and honor them but be careful that you do not give all of God's glory to the messenger because God is a jealous God. Pray about your spiritual address so that you are careful not to miss out on your spiritual mail because you made an unauthorized relocation.

Today's Sentence Prayer
Dear Lord, please align me in the right spiritual location to receive the messages you have regarding my life. In Jesus' name, I pray…Amen.

DAY 28
FREE AT LAST

John 8:36 (KJV)
If the Son therefore shall make you free, ye shall be free indeed.

You have been freed from the bondage of sin and although you are human, you do not have to stay in a prison cell that you have been set free from. Hallelujah, you are free at last!

Today's Sentence Prayer
Dear Lord, I simply want to say thank you for opening the cell doors and setting me free. In Jesus' name, I pray…Amen.

DAY 29
APPEARANCES

1 Samuel 16:7 (KJV)
But the LORD said unto Samuel, Look not on his countenance, or on the height of his stature; because I have refused him: for the LORD seeth not as man seeth; for man looketh on the outward appearance, but the LORD looketh on the heart.

God looks at the heart while somehow, we humans see everything else. The bible warns us about giving the appearance of evil because it would in fact be easy to lead babes in Christ astray or misrepresent the Kingdom of God.

Today's Sentence Prayer
Dear Lord, please help me discern the appearances I see as well as help me to be conscious of the way that I represent the Kingdom of God. In Jesus' name, I pray…Amen.

DAY 30
KEEP DREAMING

Ephesians 3:20 (KJV)
Now unto him that is able to do exceeding abundantly above all that we ask or think, according to the power that worketh in us,

---

We serve a God who is beyond able, He actually holds all power in His hands so why not dream big dreams and then go after them after all life is not a practice run but rather it's the real deal...so go for the gold.

Today's Sentence Prayer
Dear Lord, please grant me the ability to dream big dreams and then to go after those dreams as well. In Jesus' name, I pray...Amen.

DAY 31
LIGHTEN UP

Proverbs 17:22 (KJV)
A merry heart doeth good like a medicine:
but a broken spirit drieth the bones.

You are taking life and yourself much too seriously so live, laugh, love and lighten up. Enjoy this beautiful journey called life. There are funny things and people all around you including you so lighten up.

Today's Sentence Prayer
Dear Lord, please open my eyes to see the funny things in life so that my heart can stay merry. In Jesus' name, I pray...Amen.

THE SOLID FOUNDATION GROUP

Other Books to Enjoy:
www.TheSolidFoundationGroup.com

Man of Valor – 31 Day Devotional
by DeAngela S. Reid

Genre: Religion / Spirituality

Bountiful Blessings – 31 Day Devotional
by DeAngela S. Reid

Genre: Religion / Spirituality

Pieces of Her Life
by G.C. Tindley

Genre: Fiction / Erotic Fiction

Live Every Moment
by Shatanese Reese

Genre: Autobiography / Inspirational

Bullet Proof
by Bodie Quinette

Genre: Christian Non-Fiction / Self-Help

A Portrait of Virginia A. Smith
by Virginia A. Smith

Genre: Memoire / Inspirational

Poetic Motifs' Significance of 9
by Kish Andes

Genre: Poetry

How To Fade Like Griffin
by Kendrick Henderson

Genre: Trade / Educational

The Pig Who Became President
By Alana Johnson

Genre: Children's

Set Free by Truth
By Amari Johnson

Genre: Children's / Science Fiction

CheckMate
by Lex

Genre: Urban

The Cartel's Daughter Unedited
by Carmine

Genre: Urban

All are Available in Paperback or E-Book Formats
Anywhere Books Are Sold*

amazon BARNES &NOBLE   Google Play  BAM! BOOKS-A-MILLION

Your online review for any of the listed books will be greatly appreciated.

To learn more about the authors and/ or their upcoming books |or| to obtain information about becoming an author yourself, please visit our website:

www.TheSolidFoundationGroup.com

www.ingramcontent.com/pod-product-compliance
Lightning Source LLC
Chambersburg PA
CBHW050449010526
44118CB00013B/1756